REPTILE RESCUE

REPTILE

RESCUE

PEGGY THOMAS

The Science of Saving Animals

TWENTY-FIRST CENTURY BOOKS
BROOKFIELD, CONNECTICUT

FOR MY MOTHER, THE SNAKE LADY

ACKNOWLEDGMENTS

I would like to thank all the researchers and reptile specialists who shared their work with me, especially Edward Standora from the State University College at Buffalo, Marion Janusz at R.A.R.E., Robert Hay at the Department of Natural Resources Bureau of Endangered Resources in Wisconsin, Brian Bowen from the University of Florida, Gainesville, John Dayton and Sonia Mumford at the New England Aquarium, Lynn Kirkland at the St. Augustine Alligator Farm, Rick Hudson at the Fort Worth Zoo, and Wendy Taylor at the National Marine Fisheries Service.

Cover photograph courtesy of © Fritz Polking/Peter Arnold, Inc.
Photographs courtesy of Animals Animals/Earth Scenes: pp. 2 (© Zig Leszczynski), 10 (© Zig Leszczynski), 12 (© C. C. Lockwood), 23 (© Zig Leszczynski), 29 (© Fred Whitehead), 32 (© Michael Andrews); Peter Arnold, Inc.: pp. 6 (© Frederick J. Dodd), 22 (© Fred Bruemmer), 24 (© Martin Wendler); © 1996 Gary Braasch: p. 16; Dr. Frank Paladino, Purdue University: p. 19; The National Audubon Society Collection/Photo Researchers, Inc.: pp. 28 (© John Mitchell), 31 (© Chet Tussey), 43 (© Kenneth W. Fink), 46 (bottom © Stephen Dalton), 51 (© 1990 Alok Kavan); S. Knapp, New England Aquarium: p. 34; Jim Darlington: p. 36; R.A.R.E. Inc.: pp. 39 (Judy Perkowski), 40 (bottom: Judy Perkowski); Charles Tambiah: p. 46 (top); Jessie Cohen, National Zoological Park, Smithsonian Institution © Smithsonian Institution: p. 48; © Jim Stamates.com: p. 54; Matt Lorne, Nevada Department of Transportation: p. 55; N.O.A.A.: p. 57 (Ian K. Workman)

Library of Congress Cataloging-in-Publication Data
Thomas, Peggy.
Reptile rescue / by Peggy Thomas.
p.   cm. — (The Science of saving animals)
Includes bibliographical references (p.   ) and index.
Summary: Examines how scientists attempt to protect and monitor various reptiles around the world like alligators, turtles, and iguanas through radio tracking, captive breeding, habitat conservation, and poaching control.
ISBN 0-7613-3232-4 (lib. bdg.)
1. Reptiles Juvenile literature. 2. Wildlife conservation Juvenile literature.
[1. Reptiles. 2. Wildlife conservation.]
I. Title. II. Series: Thomas, Peggy. Science of saving animals.
QL644.2.T5   2000
333.95'716—dc21   99-37435   CIP

Published by Twenty-First Century Books
A Division of The Millbrook Press, Inc.
2 Old New Milford Road
Brookfield, Connecticut 06804
www.millbrookpress.com

CONTENTS

The toothy jaws of an American crocodile

1 WHY SAVE REPTILES?

As tourists watch, an alligator cruises silently up the center of the canal, no fence between the 6-foot (2-meter) -long reptile and the people. On the opposite shore, a smaller alligator warms itself in the sunlight.

These reptiles rule in Georgia's Okeefenokee swamp, where alligators are thriving. But at the southern tip of Florida where freshwater meets the ocean, the American crocodile struggles to survive. It's one of the rarest reptiles in the United States, and it is disappearing fast along with the timber rattlesnake, Kemp's ridley sea turtle, and many other reptile species.

COLD AND SCALY

There are more than 6,000 species of reptiles that come in all shapes and sizes, from 20-foot (6-meter) -long crocodiles to turtles that fit in the palm of a hand, from lumbering sea turtles to desert-baked lizards. They are grouped in four categories, or orders: the crocodilians (alligators, crocodiles, and gharials); lizards and snakes;

turtles and tortoises; and the tuatara. But they all share a few characteristics, such as a specialized heart unique to reptiles. They cannot produce their own body heat, which is why reptiles are called cold-blooded animals. A better term is ectotherm, meaning outside heat, because reptiles are solar-powered, relying on the sun for warmth and energy. Most reptiles also have scales covering their bodies and claws.

THE ROLE OF REPTILES

Reptiles, like all animals, are an important part of the ecosystem in which they live. They help maintain the environment by eating rats and other rodents that spread disease and plague farmers' crops. They're the pest-control specialists of the animal world. There is evidence that the decline of rattlesnakes in New Mexico is partly responsible for the rise of a deadly disease called the hanta virus that is spread by a rampant rodent population.

Reptiles don't just keep other animal populations down; they help some species survive. Some seeds cannot germinate without going through the digestive system of an animal. Plant-eating reptiles such as iguanas spread seeds throughout their habitat. The cool wallowing holes that crocodilians excavate for themselves become life-saving pools during the dry season, the only source of water for other reptiles and birds, amphibians, fish, and mammals. In the desert, the gopher tortoise digs long, deep tunnels that form underground apartments for more than 360 different species of insects, snakes, rodents, and other animals. If the gopher tortoise disappeared, many animals would be homeless and exposed to the heat. Removing reptiles from their habitat may cause problems that scientists haven't even discovered yet.

"As with all creatures in nature, the loss of one can have consequences that are contrary to maintaining a healthy ecosystem," said Robert Hay, a biologist for the Department of Natural Resources Bureau of Endangered Resources in Wisconsin. "We cannot afford to assume that any species, plant or animal, are here by accident. In fact, we should assume they are all here to perform valuable functions."

The American Crocodile (*Crocodylus acutus*)

There are only about 500 American crocodiles in the United States. They live on the edge of fresh and salt water in the southern tip of Florida, competing for habitat against human development. The crocodile can grow up to 20 feet (6 meters) in length, and is distinguished from the American alligator by its pointed snout and visible teeth.

PROTECTING A PEST

If reptiles are so important, than why aren't more people rallying to "Save the Snakes"? It's because reptiles have gotten a bad rap. They've been linked with dangerous dinosaurs and associated with city-stomping Godzilla. Glittering lizards, and silent, slithering snakes have given people the shivers for centuries. Except for slow-moving turtles and tortoises, reptiles have been low on most people's list of cute animals. But as one curator at the St. Augustine Alligator Farm in Florida said, "It's about time reptiles got some sympathy."

That's easier said than done. Throughout history reptiles have been viewed as pests, food, and even fancy footwear. In the last half of the twentieth century, an estimated 20 million crocodilians were killed for their hides.

In addition, the pet trade has severely depleted wild reptile populations. In just one year, more than 50,000 freshwater map turtles that live along the Mississippi River were taken out of the wild and sent to Europe and Asia to be sold as pets. Every state can quote similar disturbing statistics.

In Wisconsin, the timber rattlesnake was, and in some people's minds still is, considered a pest. Until 1975, there was a bounty (a fee paid to hunters to kill pest species) of up to $5 a tail in an effort to keep the poisonous snake "under control." Thousands of snakes were killed each year. Rattlesnake hunting was not only a job, but also part of the culture.

This is the Pine Barrens color variation of the timber rattlesnake.

In the 1980s scientists discovered that decades of slaughter was pushing this shy snake close to extinction. In an area where once a hundred snakes could be found, there were now only a few.

In 1995, when scientists proposed listing the timber rattlesnake as a threatened species in Wisconsin, there was a huge outcry from the public who feared the poisonous snakes, as well as from the government that felt the plan was too controversial. Legislator DuWayne Johnsrud even boasted, "We've been working very hard to make them [rattlesnakes] extinct, why would we want to stop now."

So how do scientists protect species that so many people have been taught to hate? "Our only hope is through education," biologist Robert Hay said. "It's going to take time, but hopefully we'll be able to make some progress before it's too late for the snake."

The struggle continues even though the timber rattlesnake was listed as a "Protected Animal" in 1998, making it illegal to kill or capture a rattler except in a life-threatening situation involving humans or domestic animals. To keep those instances down, Hay and his staff teach people how to avoid dangerous situations, and to share the environment with snakes. They hold workshops on how to distinguish a poisonous rattler from a nonpoisonous snake, how to landscape to discourage snakes, and how to safely capture a rattlesnake so it can be relocated. They are eager to teach people that rattlesnakes are shy, reluctant to strike unless provoked, and vital in keeping rodent populations in woodland areas in check.

The job of educating the public is difficult and ongoing. The fear is still there, and people probably will continue to practice what Johnsrud calls a "shoot, shovel, and shut up" policy.

"The reality is no matter what we do with the law, we will not change opinions with it," Robert Hay said. But we will change opinions with knowledge.

WHAT MAKES REPTILES SO VULNERABLE?

The greatest threat to most reptiles is loss of habitat. Land that was wild is being made into farmland and communities. Wetlands are drained for human use, leaving crocodilians and turtles to compete for smaller patches of water. It is estimated that the timber rattlesnake has lost as much as 95 percent of its habitat.

Pesticides and other chemicals that seep into the ground often contaminate the wilderness that remains. Scientists who study the environment monitor reptile species because reptiles are quick to show signs of disease and life-threatening mutations due to pollution, making them good indicators of a habitat's health.

Another contaminant to many ecosystems is the invasion of foreign species that take over a habitat. Small tropical islands once ruled by reptiles have been overrun with rats, mongooses, domesticated pigs, dogs, and cats that eat reptile eggs and hatchlings.

Fishnets are responsible for the deaths of many sea turtles each year. This loggerhead turtle has become entangled near Roatan in the Caribbean.

Marine reptiles such as sea turtles face threats on land and sea. On shore, cars, bright lights, and other human interference make it difficult for female sea turtles to lay their eggs. In the ocean they are threatened by commercial fishing, getting caught in nets and drowning. They suffer from oil pollution, and suffocate when they mistake plastic garbage bags for jellyfish, a favorite food.

Unfortunately the reptile's reproductive behavior is what makes them so vulnerable to environmental threats. Reptiles have long lives. Many species of turtle and tortoise live to be more than 100 years old, crocodiles live as long as people do, and snakes can live more than 20 years. Because they are so long-lived they don't reproduce very quickly. The female timber rattlesnake, for example, takes up to 11 years to reach maturity and only reproduces every 3 to 4 years.

Even when large numbers of young hatch from a sea-turtle nest, or are born live from a snake mother, very few ever grow to adulthood. The survival of these species depends on longevity, but environmental changes can occur quickly. Reptiles don't have time to recover from the damage.

TEAMWORK

Fortunately, many scientists are working to rescue reptiles. It's a team effort, because one scientist or one field of study can't solve a problem that has developed over hundreds of years.

The study of reptiles and amphibians is called herpetology. Although most scientists who work with endangered reptiles are herpetologists, many others are involved in conservation strategies. Not all scientists look at the same problem in the same way. Some work on a large scale, tracking sea turtles over thousands of miles of ocean, while others study the territory inside a living cell. Some scientists map out a turtle's migration route, or an alligator's family ties, while others care for sick snakes or breed rare lizards. But all these scientists are working to ensure that reptiles have a future in the wild.

Timber Rattlesnake (*Crotalus horridus*)

Even this snake's scientific name reveals people's attitude toward it. Timber rattlers live in rocky outcroppings, open grassy areas in the spring and deciduous forests in the summer. Besides being hunted, the snake has lost most of its habitat. The yellow, brown, and rust colored snake grows to be about 4 feet (1.2 meters) long, including the tan rattle on its tail. The rattler does not stalk its food, but waits for a small animal to pass by, then uses venom to disable the prey before swallowing it whole. Today timber rattlesnakes are considered rare in 15 states and have disappeared entirely from Maine, Rhode Island, and all of Canada.

2 HOW TO TRACK A TURTLE

The foundation of any animal conservation plan is knowing as much as possible about the species: where it lives, what it eats, how it reproduces, how it interacts with its environment. But reptiles don't give up this information easily. They tend to stay underground or in hiding for weeks at a time. Sea turtles come to shore only five to ten times a year, and then for only an hour or so, long enough to lay eggs. Very little is known about the lives of many reptile species.

One of the best ways to solve the mysteries of a reptile's life is to act like a detective and follow it. That's the job of field biologists who observe and monitor wild animals in their natural habitat. Many consider themselves lucky if they can find a few individuals once or twice a year as they migrate. But what do reptiles do the rest of the time?

REPTILE RADIO

Field biologists rely on radio telemetry, or tracking, to keep tabs on an animal when it's out of sight. An animal is fitted with a small radio transmitter and then released to go about its normal activities. The transmitter is a high-tech mini radio station that plays only one tune, a "beep-beep" sent out on the airwaves at a unique frequency. The only people who can hear the tune are the field biologists with their receivers set at the same frequency. To locate small, slow-moving reptiles, they use a handheld receiver with a directional antenna that looks like the letter H lying flat. New technology now allows field biologists to follow the movements of animals once thought impossible to track.

SIGNALS FROM A SNAKE

Most people avoid stepping on snakes, but biologist Jesus Rivas tries to step on them—barefoot! It is one of the only ways to locate the largest snake in the world, the anaconda, in the swamps of Venezuela.

During one search, when Rivas felt a snake beneath his feet, he reached down into the mud and grabbed. "It won't bite unless you grab it too close to the head," he said. After he wrestled the writhing, 10-foot (3-meter) -long, 100-pound (45-kilogram) snake into a canvas bag, Rivas took it to his makeshift lab to measure and mark it with an identification number.

Rivas was conducting the first major study on anacondas to learn more about how the snakes live and use their environment. No one really knows how many anacondas are out there, or whether their populations are affected by hunters who kill anacondas for their skins.

Part of Rivas's research plan included fitting several snakes with transmitters and following them through the wet and dry seasons. Most researchers surgically implant a transmitter just under a snake's skin because a snake has no neck or limbs to attach a device to. But Rivas discovered a different way to implant a transmitter. He had a pregnant female anaconda swallow it! The transmitter would then stay in the belly of the snake throughout the pregnancy because pregnant snakes do not eat, and therefore do

Jesus Rivas catches a 12-foot (3.7-meter) -long female anaconda as part of his population study in Venezuela.

not defecate, until after the young are born. This technique is much easier on the snake than having it endure surgery.

Rivas tracked the snakes on foot, on horseback, and by ultra-light plane. The data he collected will be used to develop a sound conservation plan to regulate hunting.

MADE TO ORDER

Because reptiles come in all shapes and sizes, so do the transmitters. Each one is specially designed so that it doesn't affect the animal's normal behavior or movement. The challenge is making them small enough and designed well enough so that they stay on. Transmitters are glued to the shells of turtles and tortoises, and fixed to the top of a crocodilian's head. Lizards wear tiny harnesses on their backs. A new way to attach a transmitter to a leatherback sea turtle uses a biodegradable surgical screw that goes into the shell, a tool originally used in human operations to hold bones together.

Transmitters can provide more than just the location of the animal. Some have a temperature sensor that registers the animal's internal temperature, which tells the scientists if a reptile is in hibernation, basking in the sun, or swimming in cool water.

MIGRATION MYSTERY

As soon as a sea turtle hatches on shore it scurries to the sea to spend the rest of its life swimming in the open ocean. Males will never come to shore again, and adult females will only come back at nesting time to lay their eggs. Where do they go the rest of the time? Biologist Edward A. Standora from the State University College at Buffalo and his team of researchers decided to find out. They went to the beaches of Playa Grande, Costa Rica, to fit female leatherback turtles with transmitters. They couldn't use ordinary VHF Radio telemetry to study the leatherbacks because the signal doesn't penetrate through water, and does not work long range. Leatherbacks migrate as far south as New Zealand and north to the Arctic Circle.

By using satellite technology, Standora could study the sea turtles no matter how far they went. Leatherbacks may dive as deep as 3,200 feet (1,000 meters) for several minutes, but they surface for as long as 2 minutes—long enough for a satellite to read their position.

Anaconda (*Eunectes murinus*)

The anaconda is one of the largest nonpoisonous snakes in the world, growing up to 30 feet (9 meters) in length. It can be found in South America living primarily in or near water. The anaconda is a constrictor, which means it suffocates its prey of birds, fish, and small mammals.

Standora selected 8 female turtles that had come ashore in the middle of the night to lay their Ping-Pong-ball-size eggs. "We'd spend most of the night on the beach walking many miles looking for what looks like tank tracks in the sand where a female crawled up," Standora said. "At that point we could scare her and she'd turn around and leave the beach, so we'd wait until she had dug her nest. Once the eggs started dropping out, then we'd run up there and start taking measurements and temperatures."

A female won't lay all of her eggs at once. She'll lay perhaps 100 one night and then return every ten days or so to lay 100 more until she's finished. Standora was particularly interested in the females that were on the beach for the last time. These were the turtles that would be starting their long migration. In order to identify these females, Standora used an ultrasound device that produces an image of the inside of the turtle to show if it was carrying any more eggs. It's the same technology used in hospitals to view a human baby inside a mother's body.

Once a female was selected, the researchers took only 19 minutes to attach the tracking device. First a hole was drilled into the back edge of the turtle's leathery shell. A 12-inch (30-centimeter) -long coated, metal cable was inserted through the shell and attached to a foam tube that is watertight and floats.

The actual transmitter fits snugly inside the foam tube, and is only a couple of inches long. The antenna sticks out the top of the tube. The entire apparatus is 2.5 feet (0.8 meter) long and is designed to remain on the surface of the water while the turtle

Leatherback Sea Turtle (*Dermochelys coriacea*)

There are 8 species of sea turtle, and the leatherback is the largest, growing up to 10 feet (3 meters) long and weighing more than 1,500 pounds (681 kilograms). Instead of having hard scales on its shell, it has a firm leathery skin with seven ridges running from front to back. It feeds primarily on jellyfish.

At Playa Grande, Costa Rica, Dr. Standora holds the transmitter attached to an adult female leatherback turtle that is making her way back to the Pacific Ocean.

swims just below. The cable has a breakaway feature to prevent turtles from becoming trapped underwater if the device becomes snagged. The breakaway feature also ensures that the turtle won't carry the device forever.

The tracking unit was set at a specific frequency and programmed to turn itself on and off at specific times each day. Every time the turtle rose to the surface to take a breath, the attached transmitter sent a signal to a satellite, which calculated the location of the turtle and relayed the message to a ground station. Standora could access the information from a computer anywhere in the world.

Sending a Signal—Satellite Technology

There are hundreds of satellites orbiting in space that are used for science, communications, and by the military. A pair of weather satellites follows a path over each pole as the Earth rotates beneath them, taking photographs of weather systems all over the world. They also carry a French tracking system called Argos that receives signals beamed up from an animal's transmitter. The two satellites work together to locate the position of the signal from anywhere on the planet.

Another system, called Global Positioning System (GPS), uses satellites originally launched into space by the United States military. GPS receives signals from 24 satellites, making it more accurate than Argos, able to pinpoint a transmitter's location to within a few feet.

In the future, scientists hope to use low-orbit telephone satellites, so that someday they can phone the animal's transmitter and find out where it is.

Of the 8 turtles tagged, one lost its transmitter after only three days. Turtle #1109B traveled the longest distance—1,737 miles (2,795 kilometers) until Standora lost transmission. By keeping track of these and other turtles' travels over four years, Standora and his crew made an important discovery. They learned that every year sea turtles swim the same pathways, or corridors, in the sea.

Now that scientists and conservationists know about these well-traveled routes, they can design conservation plans to protect the turtles as well as other animals that use the same corridors. Most conservation efforts so far have focused on sea-turtle nesting beaches and protecting the eggs. Now laws can focus on regulating net fishing in the corridors, or altering shipping traffic in sea-turtle areas. As Standora pointed out, "We can't effectively protect the entire ocean, but now we can target important areas—these migratory corridors."

3 WILDLIFE DETECTIVES

Where do those exotic lizards, tortoises, and snakes that you see in the pet shops come from? Some are raised by reputable breeders, but others are brought into this country illegally.

The market for exotic pets is very profitable. It is fueled by buyers in this country. Poachers as far away as Africa and Southeast Asia scour the jungles scooping up scaly creatures by the thousands. The most popular reptile pet in the United States is the green iguana, and more than 800,000 are taken from the wild each year. So many rare Egyptian tortoises have been poached that only one small, wild population still exists.

Once they are captured, the reptiles are smuggled into the United States under horrible conditions. Turtles are cruelly taped inside their shells, and snakes are balled into tight bundles of 100 to 200. These tropical reptiles are left to starve or freeze in cold cargo bays during the trip. Most of them die before they are ever unpacked.

Wild Egyptian tortoises are very scarce. This photograph was taken in the Negev Desert, Israel.

CATCHING PET POACHERS

Poachers in the United States don't have to go far to find their prey. Armed with walking sticks, flashlights, pillowcases, and coolers, poachers creep into our national parks at night to commit crimes against wildlife. People forget that our native species of rattlesnake and gopher tortoise, among others, are precious to collectors in Europe and Asia and greedily gathered up and shipped out by poachers. Wildlife agents believe that at one time as many as 200 snakes each night were being taken out of Big Bend National Park in Texas.

Several species of rattlesnake are now endangered partly because of poaching, and so are many freshwater turtles, such as the map turtle and the bog turtle. It is not just taking the animal that is devastating to species, but how they are captured. Some poachers destroy important habitats with crowbars. They use dynamite to dig up snake burrows, or pour gasoline down tortoise holes.

To catch the criminals, park rangers went undercover in one investigation code-named Operation Rockcut. Pretending to be poachers and buyers, the rangers identified whole groups of poachers who would come into the park late at night and fill their sacks and coolers with snakes. Thirty men were arrested, and Operation Rockcut put poachers on alert that reptile rustling doesn't pay.

TURTLE SOUP AND SNAKE SNEAKERS

Not all reptiles poached in the United States and other countries are being sold as pets. Many are slaughtered to be made into gruesome souvenirs, clothing, and food. In this country, freshwater turtles once easily found in creeks and rivers can now be found for sale in Asian food markets. The sale of turtles for food is common in Southeast Asia, but the practice has devastated all of the native species, some of which are nearly extinct. Snakes are hunted more than any other reptile; their skins are made into purses, belts, shoes, wallets, food, and other commercial products. Scientists

Map turtles are one of many reptile species endangered because of poaching.

This Brazilian poacher has illegally killed a caiman so that he may sell the parts.

believe that snakes may be dying out faster than any other group of vertebrates (animals with backbones).

To slow the trade and prevent rare animals from becoming extinct, a treaty called the Convention on International Trade in Endangered Species (CITES) was written in the early 1970s and signed by more than 140 countries. But there are still many poachers selling reptile parts to dealers. Fortunately, there are also wildlife agents trying to catch these criminals.

CRIME DETECTIVES

In order to convict poachers, the agents have to know which species of snake or crocodile was killed to make the product. Some species are protected by law and some aren't. But it's not easy to identify a skin when the item is a small watchband. So wildlife agents turn the job of identification over to the scientists at the National Fish and Wildlife Forensics Laboratory in Ashland, Oregon. "Forensic" means the scientific work that the lab does can be used in a court of law. The lab's main goal is to identify the species of the animal, determine the cause of death, and link the suspect to both the victim (reptile) and the crime scene.

More than 200 federal fish and wildlife agents, 80 wildlife inspectors at U.S. ports of entry, as well as state and international agencies have sent evidence to the Ashland forensics lab for analysis. The forensic scientists have seen all sorts of animal products, many of which were made from reptiles—stuffed sea turtles, snakeskin sneakers, cobra skin cowboy boots, crocodile purses, and guitars made from sea-turtle shells, just to name a few.

Identifying reptile skins is the job of a trained morphologist, a scientist who studies the physical differences between animal species. Stephen Busack, a herpetologist formerly with the lab, specialized in cold-blooded animals. His work focused on the tiniest variations between reptile skins, because, as he said, there are 168 species of snake in China alone that could be made into shoes.

The color of the skin often can't be used to identify one species from another, because the skins may have been dyed. Busack looked at specific characteristics in the pattern and shape of scales, and used simple methods such as counting and measuring each scale to make the identification. Once he even ran a whole caiman skin through the photocopy machine to make a map of its bumps and features. In the future, distinguishing caimans from crocodiles and alligators will be much easier.

The forensic scientists also use a large collection of reptile skins called reference standards to identify evidence. It's much like a museum collection with examples of all different kinds of animals. If a purse, for example, appeared to be made out of a cobra skin, that evidence would be compared with a cobra skin in the reference collection in order to make a match.

If the skin proved to be that of an endangered or threatened species that is protected by CITES, the scientist would be asked to testify in a court of law. Each trial that stops an unlawful importer is a victory for wildlife conservation. As Ken Goddard, the lab's director said, "We educate one criminal at a time."

4 IT'S IN THE GENES

A tiny drop of blood can answer a lot of questions. It can tell scientists about an animal's health and who its parents are, and now it can provide clues about an animal's migration. It's all in the genes—in genetic material called DNA. The study of DNA and living cells is called genetics. The work geneticists do has solved crimes and identified missing people, and now scientists are learning how important DNA studies can be for the conservation of endangered species.

GENETIC TRACKING

Satellite tracking has led scientists to sea-turtle nesting sites and feeding grounds, but genetic tracking is making the connection between turtle populations around the world by showing how they are genetically related.

The loggerhead sea turtles that nest on the southeastern beaches of the United States are listed as a threatened species. Their populations have been

DNA

Inside every living cell is the blueprint of life—genetic material called DNA (deoxyribonucleic acid). DNA contains instructions for how an organism is made. It controls the length of a lizard's tail, the color of a snake's stripes, and the size of a sea turtle's shell. DNA is coiled in the cell's nucleus in threadlike strands that are called chromosomes. Individual sections of the chromosomes are called genes. Every animal gets half of its DNA from its mother and half from its father.

A blood sample is drawn from a snake for DNA testing.

Also inside every cell is a different kind of DNA called mitochondrial DNA (mDNA) The mitochondria is the powerhouse of the cell. The mDNA inside the mitochondria comes from only one parent—the mother, so scientists can use it to trace back through a family to link animals with their mother, grandmother, and so on.

decreasing since the 1970s. Part of the problem occurs right on the beach; bright lights, beach traffic, and litter disturb egg-laying, and predators take most of the hatchlings before they ever reach the water. Until recently it was a mystery as to where the surviving young turtles went after they hatched from U.S. beaches, and what deadly threats they encountered.

Turtles that nest along a particular coastline have a distinctive mDNA pattern, different from that of turtles that nest on beaches in other parts of the world. This is because females return to nest on the same beaches every year.

Geneticist Brian Bowen from the University of Florida, Gainesville, studied mDNA extracted from blood taken from female sea turtles as they came ashore to nest, from tissue samples collected from dead turtles pulled aboard fishing boats, as well as from turtles plucked right out of the ocean. As a geneticist, much of Bowen's work is conducted in a lab, but sometimes he gets a chance to work out in the field to collect his own samples. Once he and his colleagues hitched a ride with Mexican fishermen off the coast of Baja, California, looking for loggerhead sea turtles dining on large concentrations of red crab.

When the fishermen maneuvered the boat next to a turtle basking at the surface, Bowen jumped overboard, grabbed the turtle by the shell, and steered it toward the boat. The trick was getting the turtle and the researcher back in the boat before the arrival of sharks that are attracted by the feeding turtles. In the boat Bowen used a needle to collect a few drops of blood from a vein in the turtle's neck. It's a simple and quick procedure that's even been used on hatchlings. Then the turtle was returned to the sea unharmed.

A loggerhead sea turtle comes ashore on Cumberland Island, Georgia.

Back in the lab at the University of Florida the samples were processed using a special method called polymerase chain reaction (PCR). PCR can take tiny fragments of DNA and copy it a million times, so that it can be examined easily. "Then it's fed into one of three machines called automated DNA sequencers, which can break down the DNA into its smallest units," said Bowen. These amazing machines don't look like much—about the size of a small microwave oven—but they can do as much work in three days as it would take one person six years to do by hand.

By studying the mDNA, Bowen matched turtles from halfway around the world to their nesting sites. He compared data with a French scientist and discovered that most of the loggerheads that drowned in fishing nets in the Mediterranean Sea had originally come from beaches in Florida, Georgia, and South Carolina. The fact that 20,000 to 50,000 loggerheads died in the Mediterranean each year helped to explain why fewer and fewer loggerheads were returning to nest in the United States.

Bowen's genetic research provided valuable evidence that government officials needed to be able to protect these turtles. In 1982 the United Nations established the Convention of the Law of the High Seas, which states, in part, that if a country takes care of an animal population during its developmental stages (like nesting) then they have jurisdiction over that animal even out on the high seas. "Once we can demonstrate that fishing activities, like drift net fishing, affect the natural resources [animals] of specific countries, then these laws apply," Bowen said.

Bowen is hopeful that another genetic study will prevent the killing of hawksbill sea turtles near Cuba. The hawksbill's shell has been used to make jewelry, eyeglass frames, guitar picks, and other ornaments, and the Cuban government wants to make it legal to hunt them in their waters. However, genetic studies proved that the turtles the Cubans would be harvesting belong to nesting areas in other countries, and should also be protected under the Law of the High Seas.

A school of jacks swims around a hawksbill sea turtle in the South Pacific Ocean.

FINDING A NEW SPECIES

DNA not only identifies populations, but can also identify a new subspecies. In 1990 a group of scientists set out to collect data on the rare and unusual tuatara that lives on islands near New Zealand. The researchers scrambled through the night in search of tuataras hunting for food. The tuataras they found were scooped up and taken back to camp, where they were photographed and measured. A few drops of blood were drawn from the tail, then the tuataras were taken back to where they were captured.

Geneticists looked at the DNA in the blood samples and developed a DNA "fingerprint," which is the pattern of DNA unique to an individual. They discovered that all tuataras are not alike. One group of tuataras that lived on North Brother Island had DNA that

Tuatara (*Sphenodon punctatus*)

The tuatara is the only species of the order of reptiles called Sphenodontia that lived at the time of the dinosaurs. They look much like an iguana, but they have an unusual skull structure, a primitive heart, and a bony abdominal skeleton. The teeth are part of the jaw-bone, and unlike most reptiles the tuatara has a voice. It croaks like a frog. It prefers cool temperatures, becoming most active at 50°F (10°C). An adult tuatara can be 2 feet (0.6 meter) long and can live more than 70 years. It survives on several small islands off the coast of New Zealand and rarely goes far from its burrow. It hunts at night for birds' eggs, nestlings, worms, and other small animals.

was different enough to be considered a new subspecies. There are perhaps 500 of this subspecies living on this tiny island, and conservationists are worried that a single storm or tidal wave could cause them to become extinct. So they are not only a new subspecies, but are also a new endangered subspecies.

5 OPEN WIDE AND SAY AHHH!

In a tank the size of a small hot tub, a Kemp's ridley sea turtle swam in a circle, poking its nose up to the surface of the water. This rare sea turtle was a patient in the Critical Care Unit at the New England Aquarium where veterinarians were trying to warm its body.

During the summer this sea turtle, like hundreds of others, visited northern waters to feed on the rich food supply. Sea turtles usually migrate to warmer waters before winter. Those that do not make the journey in time become "cold stunned." This turtle was found stranded on a beach, cold, dehydrated, and sick. "Every individual turtle is important to the species," said John Dayton, General Curator and Director of Animal Husbandry at the New England Aquarium. "There are fewer than 1,000 nesting females left in the wild."

This cold-stunned turtle needed round-the-clock care while it was being slowly warmed up. Its body temperature, which normally should be around 80°F (27°C), had fallen to a chilly 55°F (13°C). Veterinarians

Veterinarian Andy Stamper examines a rehabilitating Kemp's ridley sea turtle at the New England Aquarium in Boston, Massachusetts.

monitored its progress and gave it medicine for a bad case of pneumonia. When the turtle gained a few more pounds, it was released into warmer waters. "Working with sea turtles is very rewarding," said Sonia Mumford, the aquarium's staff veterinarian. "You really feel you're making a difference."

Veterinarians help threatened species one animal at a time, and for animals like the Chinese alligator that is almost extinct in the wild, or the rare Kemp's ridley sea turtle, every individual is important. As they work with captive reptiles, vets learn more about an animal's physiology (how an animal's body works), the spread of disease, and what an animal needs to stay healthy—information that is crucial for dealing with wild reptiles and developing conservation plans.

Vets diagnose sick animals with some of the same sophisticated medical tests and equipment that doctors use on people. "There is nothing that is done to humans that can't be done to animals," said John Dayton. They've had to truck sick sea turtles to a nearby hospital in order to use the CAT scan and X-ray equipment. But the best way to tell when a captive reptile is ill is by watching its behavior. A change in eating habits and activities can be the first sign of trouble.

ILL ALLIGATORS

Every other Monday is vet day at the St. Augustine Alligator Farm in Florida, an important breeding center for rare and endangered crocodilians. Veterinarians from the University of Florida, Gainesville, arrive in a truck loaded with equipment. They practice preventive medicine, which means they try to keep the animals in the proper environment and on an appropriate diet to prevent them from getting sick. Most of these house calls are routine, but sometimes the vet faces a medical emergency.

In 1995 a mysterious illness spread through two of the pens at the farm. "The first alligator to die was one of the larger and older ones that had been there for many years," said Lynn Kirkland, curator of the alligator farm. Because of its age, its death was not a big surprise. But more dead alligators were found—four in just one day. It was a major cause for concern because the alligator farm was set up in a series of large open pens, with an even larger swamp area where alligators and turtles swam freely. A disease could spread quickly from one pen to another and infect the more rare crocodilians.

Kirkland called the vets immediately. They quickly got to work, taking blood samples from all the alligators in the infected areas, and moving the sick ones into a holding pen to prevent the disease from spreading.

Dr. Avery Bennett and his crew hoisted dead alligators into the truck and took them to the university so that the bodies could be examined. Tissue samples were tested for viruses, bacteria, and poisons, but test results were inconclusive. "We didn't have a consis-

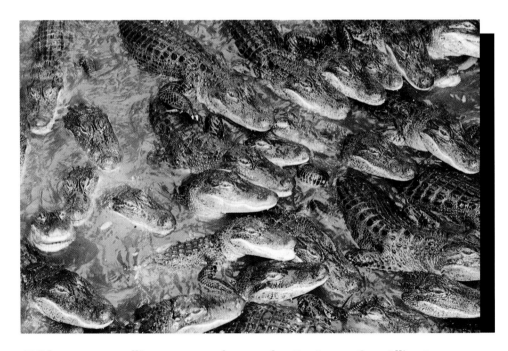

With so many alligators together at the St. Augustine Alligator Farm, you can understand why the outbreak of mycoplasma spread so quickly. It was important to diagnose the disease fast.

tent picture," Dr. Bennett said. They called a meeting of vets, pathologists—scientists who study disease—and other specialists to diagnose the problem. "All the sick alligators had pneumonia and infections in their joints," said Dr. Bennett. These symptoms reminded them of a bacterial disease called mycoplasma that is common in tortoises. "We went back and found it," he said—a respiratory infection related to mycoplasma that spread from one alligator to another through close contact within the pools. By this time more than 100 animals had died.

To prevent other crocodilians from getting sick, Kirkland, the vets, and the keepers had to give the surviving alligators injections of antibiotics once a week. "At first we would enter the pen and manually restrain the alligator's mouth before giving it the shot, but then the animals got so used to us we could just slip up behind them and jab them in the leg. They had that here-we-go-again attitude," said Kirkland.

Today at the alligator farm you can see a healthy population of alligators and some of the rarest crocodilians that continue to grow and breed because they were saved from a potentially devastating disease.

A R.A.R.E. TREAT

Taking care of sick animals is a nonstop, 24-hour-a-day job. Just ask reptile specialist and certified rehabilitator Marion Janusz, who founded R.A.R.E., the Reptile Adoption, Rehabilitation & Education Center, in Buffalo, New York.

Most of the reptiles she works with are former pets. Many reptile pet owners start out loving their small snake only to find that it grows to be 6 feet (1.8 meters) long and eats live rats, or they realize that it's not easy to raise a healthy iguana. Most pets die too soon, but some lucky lizards end up at R.A.R.E.

Some people think that taking care of unwanted pets does nothing for the conservation of animals, but in a way it does. The enormous illegal trade in reptile pets has devastated many wild populations. One factor that fuels the business is people's belief that reptiles are emotionless, disposable pets. Taking care of unwanted pets plays an important role in altering people's perceptions. As Janusz pointed out, "It's important for people to realize that lizards and snakes have feelings of pain and comfort just like other animals do." In the long run, changing people's attitudes will eventually make conservation much easier.

A rehabilitator is a trained person who nurses wild animals back to health, and in some cases may release them back into the wild. Not just anyone can become one; you have to pass an exam and become certified by the state. Janusz used to work with birds and mammals until she realized that there was a real need for a reptile specialist, because so few people know about reptiles. Even vets trained to work on cats and dogs are usually not well versed in dealing with tortoises or iguanas.

Janusz is not a vet, but she works closely with one, Dr. Carl P. Tomaschki. She learns from Dr. Tomaschki as they go along, just as many other professionals do who work with exotic animals. "Each animal I get teaches me something new," she said. Occasionally Janusz accompanies Dr. Tomaschki to perform necropsies on dead animals to learn how they died. A necropsy on a python, for example, teaches Janusz how the snake's body functions, which will help her the next time she rehabilitates a python.

The first thing Janusz does when a new animal is brought to her is give it a checkup. She looks inside its mouth, inspects it for ticks and mites, and checks the animal's overall body tone. Then she leaves it alone to rest quietly. "It's very stressful for an animal to be

Wood Turtle (Clemmys insculpta)

This 6- to 8-inch (15- to 20-centimeter) -long freshwater turtle has a shell that looks like polished wood. It lives along forested rivers and streams, eating berries, plants, and insects. It is listed as threatened in some areas.

Marion Janusz, of R.A.R.E., examines a boa constrictor. All the patients at R.A.R.E. are checked daily.

moved from place to place," Janusz said, so she gives it time to relax and get used to its new home. This also gives Janusz time to watch and learn how the animal behaves. Janusz firmly believes that animals often can heal themselves if their stress is reduced, they are kept at a proper temperature, and given proper nutrition. When the animals are healthy they will be adopted out to someone who has learned to care for them.

Although most of her rehabilitated animals are former pets, Janusz also receives wild animals that have had run-ins with

The outdoor turtle garden at
R.A.R.E. is the warm-weather
home for several different
species of turtles and tortoises.
At right, a sulcata tortoise
enjoys a sunny day.

humans. One of them in her care, Woody, a wood turtle, was nibbling on some greens and didn't seem bothered by a cracked shell. It had been hit by a car, a common fate for many freshwater turtles. Wood turtles travel as far as 2 miles (3 kilometers) from their water habitat, crossing many roads on their way. They're fast for turtles, with a top speed of 0.2 mile, or 1,056 feet (0.3 kilometer or 300 meters) per hour, but they can't compete with traffic. Janusz repaired Woody's shell with a patch made of epoxy, a strong, resin-like glue, and fiberglass tape. The patch will stay on until Janusz is certain that the crack has healed completely and there is no danger of infection. Then she'll release Woody back to its natural habitat.

In another enclosure, a California desert tortoise with a rugged bumpy shell basks under a heat lamp. Like many unusual pets, this one was illegal to own, and had possibly been taken from the wild. The tortoise was confiscated by authorities because it is a protected species, threatened in its natural habitat. This desert tortoise can't go back to the wild because it might harbor a disease that could harm wild tortoises, or change the genetic makeup of a wild population. But it will help in the conservation of its species by making more desert tortoises in a captive-breeding program at the Bronx Zoo, New York.

6 LONESOME GEORGE'S LEGACY

Lonesome George is the last of his kind. But he doesn't seem to notice as he slowly munches greens in his pen at the Charles Darwin Research Center in the Galápagos Islands. George is the last saddleback tortoise from Pinta Island. There are other kinds, or subspecies, of Galápagos tortoise, but none just like George. Thousands of tortoises once lived on Pinta Island, but when scientists searched in 1971, George was the only one they could find.

During the last 200 years more than 100,000 Galápagos tortoises have been killed by whalers and settlers for meat and oil. Along with settlers came rats and pigs that ate tortoise eggs and hatchlings, as well as goats and mules that competed for food and trampled nests. Before man's arrival, there were several hundred thousand tortoises on the islands, but today there are fewer than 15,000. Scientists are determined to keep the remaining tortoise subspecies from suffering George's fate by giving young tortoises a head start.

TORTOISE NURSERY

Wild giant tortoises mate during the rainy season, between January and June. Sometime between June and December the females lay their eggs, and rangers search the islands for their tennis-ball-size eggs tucked away in nests.

Each egg is marked with a number and taken back to the station where they are kept in incubators the size of shoe boxes, and warmed by the sun. Captive rearing the tortoise gives it a better chance for survival. More eggs hatch in the incubators, and more young survive to adulthood, than would survive without people's help.

In four to eight months when the eggs hatch, researchers and volunteers at the center paint the egg's number on the shell of the hatchling. The number is recorded along with the baby's weight and measurements. At birth a tortoise weighs less than one thousandth of what an adult weighs, making them an easy meal for rats, wild dogs, and cats. The nursery is a much safer place during this dan-

A Galápagos tortoise on Hood Island in the Galápagos

gerous time in a wild tortoise's life. In three or four years it will be big enough to be taken back to its island to live out the rest of its long, long life. So far, nearly 2,000 tortoises have been returned to the wild.

LIZARD LOVE

The Hope Zoo in Jamaica has set up a head-start program to save one of the world's most endangered lizards. The Jamaican iguana was thought to be extinct since 1940. Then in June 1990 a pig hunter and his dog cornered a male iguana in a remote part of Jamaica called Hellshire Hills. After a thorough search, it was estimated that at least 15 iguanas lived in the forest, making the Jamaican iguana the most endangered lizard in the world. Since then two nesting sites have been discovered, and there may be between 50 to 200 iguanas in the wild. This small population living in a shrinking habitat is threatened daily by mongooses that prey on the eggs and young. It wouldn't survive for long without some help.

Since 1991 scientists have collected iguana eggs from the nest sites and have hand-reared them. Just like the tortoise head-start program, the iguanas are kept in ten pens according to age. "There are about 80 kids in head-start that will eventually be released," said Rick Hudson, Assistant Curator of reptiles at the Fort Worth Zoo in Texas, and also the species coordinator for the Rock Iguana Species Survival Plan. "Twenty have already been released."

But there is another captive population located not in Jamaica, but in the United States. "The U.S. population serves as a backup against extinction." Hudson explained. "If the wild population crashes, or something wipes them out, then we have a fallback position." Then, the entire species would depend on the breeding of 22 iguanas in 6 zoos throughout the United States. This is the nucleus of the captive-breeding population.

The lizards were chosen based on DNA analysis to represent a wide range of genetic material. Ideally a breeding program is designed to maintain the same genetic diversity that exists in nature.

Building a genetically healthy population takes a lot of hard work and coordination. The Lizard Advisory Group (LAG); the American Zoo and Aquarium Association; and the Rock Iguana Species Survival Plan (SSP), work together to monitor the captive population. Not all animals have such a dedicated force working for them; only the most endangered do. The LAG and the SSP make important decisions for captive breeding, such as where the animals are housed, which animals mate, and how often. A member of the SSP committee also keeps track of each animal in a stud book, which records the gender, age, and location of the iguana as well as births and deaths. The SSP's goal is to increase the captive popula-

Genetic Diversity

An offspring gets one half of its genetic material from its mother and one half from its father. All the different genes represented in the animal population are called the gene pool, and scientists believe that a healthy population has a wide range of different genes. This is called genetic diversity. When only a few individuals of a species are left, the gene pool is smaller, and new offspring may suffer from genetic disease. To produce the healthiest offspring possible, scientists breed within an animal species only animals that are as distantly related as possible.

Compare the Jamaican iguana at the Hope Zoo in Jamaica (above) and the green iguana in Alter Do Chao in the Amazon River basin of Brazil.

Jamaican Iguana (Cyclura collei)

Jamaican iguanas are one of eight species of West Indian rock iguanas that live throughout the Caribbean islands. They grow to be 4 to 5 feet (1.2 to 1.5 meters) long, and are considered to be one of the most endangered lizards in the world. Jamaican iguanas live on the ground, eating plants such as cacti and grasses, and they play an important role in spreading seeds for many of these unusual plants.

tion to 200. But no amount of organization will work without the cooperation of the iguanas.

The Fort Worth Zoo, for example, has four Jamaican iguanas. "We've had eggs," said Hudson. "But we have not had fertile eggs. . . . They're proving slightly more difficult than some of the other rock iguanas we've worked with. We're learning as we go," adds Hudson. That's not surprising. Since the species was thought to be extinct, no one has any experience with them.

One of the most important things zoo curators learn is how to create an environment that encourages animal pairs to mate. At the Fort Worth Zoo the tropical iguanas are kept inside during the cold winters, and let out in spring. Hudson believes natural sunlight is important, as well as proper diet and individual compatibility. "We've had pairs that just didn't get along," he said. All six zoos are learning how to take care of these rare iguanas, and share their experiences through SSP committees. Hudson is optimistic that they'll soon get the conditions just right, and the Jamaican iguana population in the United States will increase, as did the captive population of another lizard, the Komodo dragon.

FRENDITY AND SOBAT

Before 1992 no zoo in the United States had successfully bred Komodo dragons, the largest lizards in the world. Success finally

Frendity and Sobat were the first pair of Komodo dragons to breed in captivity. They live in the National Zoological Park in Washington, D.C.

came with a pair of dragons, named Frendity and Sobat, at the National Zoo in Washington D.C. Like the iguanas, Sobat, the female dragon, laid many eggs. Each time, keepers would dig them up and place them in incubators so they would be safe from the predatory parents. They were all unfertilized.

Then, in 1992, keepers uncovered 26 fertile eggs. "There were so many eggs we ran out of incubators," said one reptile keeper. Ten eggs were sent to a nearby college to be incubated. They were kept in sweater boxes under heat lamps, but no one knew just how warm the eggs should be kept, or how long before they would hatch. Two hundred and thirty-seven days later the first egg hatched. Since then dozens of Komodo dragons have been born.

Komodo dragon (Varanus komodoensis)

The Komodo dragon is the largest lizard in the world, growing up to 10 feet (3 meters) long. Wild populations live on a few small islands in Indonesia where they are a protected species. Adult dragons feed on lizards, pigs, and other large animals. Juvenile dragons spend much of their time in trees, keeping out of reach of hungry adults.

CROCODILE FARMS

There are different animal breeding programs all over the world, each one specially designed for a specific species. The Madras Crocodile Bank in India has had great success breeding endangered crocodilians that are almost extinct in the wild. It is called a "bank" because the program safeguards valuable genetic diversity for the future, when there might be a habitat for these crocodilians to go back to.

The bank was started by Romulus Whitaker in 1975 with a small group of 14 endangered crocodiles—one of them was Chitra, a kind of crocodile called a mugger. Chitra had been disturbing villagers and was in danger of being shot, so she was captured and brought to the bank, where she laid more than 700 eggs. Her babies were sent to other breeding farms and zoos, and some were put back into the wild. So far more than 1,300 gharials (thin, long-nosed crocodilians) and about 1,000 saltwater crocodiles, as well as muggers, have been reintroduced into some of India's national parks.

But in other countries, a crocodile is just another farm animal, like a pig or cow. Thousands are raised in pens and slaughtered for their skins. The hides are made into wallets, shoes, and purses. Not all conservationists agree on whether this type of farming helps the endangered crocodiles. Some say that "skin farms" eliminate the need for poachers to kill animals in the wild. However, wild crocodiles will be even safer when people no longer want to wear crocodile skins.

REBUILDING THE WILD

Putting animals back into a natural habitat is the goal of head-start programs and many captive-breeding programs. Reptiles are some of the easier animals to return to the wild. With the exception of crocodiles and alligators that guard their nests, and a few other species, most reptiles don't care for their young. Reptiles run on instinct. They know how to find food, how to protect themselves, and how to find shelter when they are born, which makes them good candidates for reintroduction to the wild. Biologists who work with mammals have to teach the animals like an animal mother would to be sure that the animals have what it takes to survive on their own. But reptiles already know.

Pest Control

The number-one threat to island reptiles is foreign predators. Island reptiles once lived sheltered lives, surviving in an ecosystem where they were top predators. Then humans arrived, bringing dogs, cats, farm animals, and rats that all disturbed the delicate balance of nature.

On Jamaica and other islands in the West Indies, rats were destroying prized sugarcane crops, so in 1872 the Indian mongoose was brought in to control the rat population. They ate the rats, but also found a feast of snakes and lizards, devastating their populations and perhaps causing the extinction of many species on smaller islands.

Part of the conservation effort to protect the Jamaican iguana includes trapping mongooses. "That's something we'll be doing forever," said Rick Hudson. "There is no way we can ever eradicate the mongoose from that area. We'll always have to do some trapping. But if we can keep the mongoose numbers down in core iguana areas, the iguana should be all right."

An alligator covered in algae basks in the sun at the Madras Crocodile Bank, while another rests in the water.

To reintroduce the tuatara back to one of its former island habitats, biologists first had to make the island safe by getting rid of all the rats. Rats came to the islands as stowaways on ships. They thrived on islands where there were no large predators, and plenty of food. Rats became the top predator and the major cause of the disappearance of many reptiles, including the tuatara.

Researchers collected more than 200 eggs from 35 tuataras on North Brother Island and raised them in a head-start program. When they were large enough, 50 juvenile and 18 adults were resettled on Titi Island and placed in burrows that scientists had made just for them. Biologists were flown to the island every few weeks to check on their progress.

They found that the tuataras didn't like the homes the researchers built, and had moved out to find their own burrows. The few tuataras that had been fitted with radio transmitters had somehow wriggled out of their harnesses, but researchers managed to locate most of them and were pleased to find that the new island residents had gained weight and seemed to be doing just fine.

Land iguanas, alligators, crocodiles, Kemp's ridley sea turtles, as well as other reptile species have all been successfully put back into their natural habitats. But for many of them, survival still depends on humans who carefully choose the habitats to ensure there is ample space, food, shelter, and mates.

7 MAKING ROOM FOR REPTILES

Reptiles are running out of room. Loss of habitat is the number-one cause for endangering most animals, including reptiles. Captive breeding and keeping individual animals healthy can only be effective if there is a place for these reptiles to live.

Most reptiles don't wander too far from home, but people chopping up large tracts of land is still devastating to them. A narrow strip of road is a deadly obstacle for a slow-moving turtle, and between 500 to 1,000 snakes are killed by traffic each year on just one stretch of roadway in southern Arizona.

Habitats are also lost because they are changed from wet to dry, from forest to fields, or from meadows to backyards. More than one half of this country's swamps and marshes have already been drained to make way for roads, houses, and businesses.

In the past, conservation plans were created for one individual species, but current wildlife management strategies focus on preserving habitats and ecosystems. Setting aside land remains top priority, but ecologists, scientists who study the interaction between animals, people, and their habitat, are devising creative ways for people and reptiles to live together.

A HOME FOR MOJAVE MAX

The desert tortoise looks out of place amid the glitzy neon signs of Las Vegas, but this species is hanging on to the habitat where it has lived for millions of years. Listed as endangered in 1989, the desert tortoise has been the center of controversy about how people and animals can live together in the same habitat. In a vast desert it would seem that there is room for everyone, but cattle graze on the same food that tortoises eat, and exotic plants are taking over native vegetation. Ranching, mining, and recreational vehicles have prompted the building of more than 34,000 miles (54,740 kilometers) of paved and dirt roads, and each road isolates pieces of habitat that once were connected. Most tortoises are crushed by vehicles because these sad-eyed, determined reptiles just can't keep pace with the growth and construction of human habitats. But they have many scientists and citizens fighting for them.

Desert tortoises don't stand a chance against motor vehicles. What might make a driver miss seeing a lumpy tortoise on a flat sand road?

The fence along Interstate 15 in Nevada was specially modified to keep tortoises off the highway. Note the wire mesh along the bottom.

In Clark County, Nevada, a conservation plan was devised to protect the land on which tortoises live, and a cartoon tortoise named Mojave Max urges people to respect the desert. Tortoise tunnels are built under roads, and farmers are paid to limit cattle grazing. Construction companies now have to create or improve habitats before they can build, and tortoises are removed from construction sites. Ecologists stand in front of bulldozers checking every crack and hole in the ground for animals that might be taking a nap in spite of the rumbling noise overhead. Tortoises pulled out of the burrows are taken to a holding pen, a homeless shelter where the tortoises stay until a new home can be found for them.

Not only has the tortoise been doing better, but so are the other 54 reptile, 41 fish, 9 amphibian, 392 bird, and 142 mammal species, and more than 800 types of plants that live in Clark County.

THE ONE THAT GOT AWAY

Even in the vast ocean, humans and animals collide. More than 150,000 sea turtles are accidentally caught and drowned in shrimp nets every year. To minimize the problem, researchers asked themselves how they could design a net that would catch thousands of tiny shrimp while letting giant sea turtles go free?

Wendy Taylor, a gear specialist at the National Marine Fisheries Service in Pascagoula, Mississippi, was one of several people who worked on creating a new design. A gear specialist is normally concerned with designing better nets to help fishermen catch more, but for this project the goal was to let something go.

A team of gear specialists and biologists experimented with several designs before finding the right one. "Initially we tried to stop the turtles from getting into the trawl," Taylor said. "A barrier in front didn't work. Then we tried a brace of metal bars to deflect the turtles, but that wasn't successful either."

Each design was tested by putting live turtles through the nets. Finally the gear specialists devised a metal grid trapdoor inside the net. This allowed shrimp to pass through to the back of the net,

Computer Conservation

The human population is growing so fast that it's impossible to think we can protect all wild lands. But what areas do we protect, and what wild areas can we do without? Ecologists use complex computer models to try to answer these questions. They look for land with great biodiversity, a large number of different species in a given space. For example, a wild meadow has more biodiversity than a lawn because more kinds of plants and animals live in a meadow.

The computer analyzes information from various sources, starting with maps that show just plant life. By layering maps of the distribution of everything from grizzly bears to insects, ecologists can build a complete picture of an area's biodiversity, and pinpoint land that needs our protection.

This Turtle Excluder Device (TED), the Super Shooter, was tested with loggerhead sea turtles specially raised at the National Marine Fisheries Services lab in Galveston, Texas.

while the turtle's heavy body flipped it through the trapdoor and out to safety. It was called a Turtle Excluder Device, or TED, and today all trawlers in the United States are required to use one. Unfortunately, shrimpers in other countries are not.

TEDs, which are 97 percent effective at releasing turtles from nets, work for most sizes of turtle, but need to be enlarged during the season when the largest leatherback turtles are in the fishing areas. Conservationists fly over the fishing zones where they can easily spot the lumbering giants as they swim at the surface of the water. The shrimpers are then notified that it's time to modify their nets so they can fish safely in leatherback territory.

Teaching a Crocodile Manners

For years, game wardens and biologists have educated people on how to live safely with wild animals, but now they've started teaching the animals how to live safely with people.

Wardens with the Florida Game and Fresh Water Fish Commission sometimes capture an American crocodile that has chosen to live too close to people's houses. They send it to Miami's Metrozoo for 30 days, where they hope the crocodile will learn that it's best to keep away from humans.

Experiments in aversion therapy have also been conducted in Australia, where saltwater crocodiles have been known to hassle fishermen. In the past these problem crocs were killed, but Steve Irwin, of the Australian Zoo, has tried to teach the crocodile to avoid humans, which would save the lives of both people and crocodiles. Irwin's cure involved trapping the problem crocodile and giving it a night to remember. All night long Irwin and his crew drove a noisy motorboat back and forth in front of the crocodile while shining flashlights in its eyes. The next morning the crocodile was released, annoyed but unharmed. Irwin hopes that what he has heard is true, that crocodiles have long memories, and that this one will remember its bad experience and stay away from people and boats.

CITIZEN SCIENCE

Not everyone can teach crocodiles good manners, or track snakes by radio, but anyone can help reptiles. In New York State, for example, more than a thousand volunteers searched the woods and stream banks looking for reptiles and amphibians as part of the New York State Herpetology Atlas Project. "Citizen scientists" filled out a survey card for each reptile they identified, and sent the cards to the Department of Conservation (DEC) in Albany to be recorded in the atlas. This important scientific information gives herpetologists baseline data that can be compared against future studies and will be used to identify reptiles and habitats in trouble.

You can check your state environmental agency to see if volunteers are needed for similar projects, or contact your local museum or zoo for more information on reptile conservation.

You can also help rescue reptiles by following these simple guidelines. Don't buy exotic pets or take turtles, snakes, or lizards from the wild. Move turtles that are in the middle of the road to the grassy shoulder. Always put them on the side of the road they were headed for, and don't use your hands to move a snapping turtle. Scoop it up with a shovel because its bite can break fingers. Performing even the smallest rescue can help an entire species. Remember, there are threatened and endangered animals in our own backyards.

Conservation is ongoing. It's not a task that will ever be finished, or a single problem that can be solved. The research discussed in this book is only a fraction of the work that is being done to rescue reptiles. For every piece of data a scientist records, more is needed. Every question scientists answer about an animal's natural history leads to a dozen more. There is more work to do.

A REPTILE SUCCESS STORY

By the 1960s the American alligator was hunted to near extinction. Much of its wetland world had been drained and turned into human habitat. As the people population grew, the alligators declined.

In 1967 the alligator was listed as an endangered species (under a law that came before the Endangered Species Act). The U.S. Fish and Wildlife Service and state agencies cracked down on poachers and created wetland reserves. People learned to respect alligators, and they made a complete recovery. Their populations grew so large that in some areas wildlife agents control their numbers.

The rescue of the American alligator is truly a success story, one that can be repeated for other endangered reptiles.

GLOSSARY

DNA—deoxyribonucleic acid, the molecule in a cell that contains coded genetic information

ectotherm—literally, outside heat, which refers to animals, including reptiles, that rely on the environment to regulate their body temperature

forensic science—a field of science devoted to producing evidence that may be used in a court of law

genetics—the science of heredity and they way living things vary

herpetology—the scientific study of reptiles and amphibians

mDNA—specialized DNA found in the mitochondria of cells. It is inherited only from the mother

morphology—the scientific study of the physical differences between animal species

necropsy—an animal autopsy

Polymerase Chain Reaction—a laboratory procedure that enhances fragments of DNA so that it can be analyzed more easily

subspecies—a separation of a species based on geography or physical differences

telemetry—the use of technology to track an animal's movements

FURTHER READING

For more information on reptiles and how scientists work, check out these and other books.

Bjorndal, Karen A., ed. *Biology and Conservation of Sea Turtles.* Washington, D.C.: Smithsonian Institution Press, 1995.

Ernst, Carl H., and George R. Zug. *Snakes in Question.* Washington, D.C.: Smithsonian Institution Press, 1996.

Levy, Charles. *Endangered Species—Crocodiles and Alligators.* Secaucus, NJ: Chartwell Books, 1991.

Lutz, Richard L., and others. *Komodo, the Living Dragon.* Salem: Dimi Press, 1996.

Manaster, Jane. *Horned Lizards.* Austin: University of Texas Press, 1997.

Montgomery, Sy. *The Snake Scientist.* Boston: Houghton Mifflin, 1999.

Phillips, Pamela. *The Great Ridley Rescue.* Missoula, MT: Mountain Press, 1988.

Tesar, Jenny. *What on Earth Is a Tuatara?* Woodbridge, CT: Blackbirch Press, 1994.

INTERNET INFORMATION

Sites on the Internet change quickly. However, here are a few sites you can contact to learn more about reptiles and conservation.

Charles Darwin Research Station at http://fcdarwin.org.ec/

For information on reptile pet care check out www.Kingsnake.com

National Wildlife Federation at www.nwf.org/nwf

Sea Turtle Conservation at www.seaturtle.org

Look up your favorite zoo on www.ZooNet.com

INDEX